The Case

For

ISO 27001

The Case

For

ISO 27001

ALAN CALDER

IT Governance Publishing

Publisher's Note

Every possible effort has been made to ensure that the information contained in this book is accurate at the time of going to press, and the publishers and the author cannot accept responsibility for any errors or omissions, however caused. No responsibility for loss or damage occasioned to any person acting, or refraining from action, as a result of the material in this publication can be accepted by the publisher or the author.

First published in the United Kingdom in 2005 by IT Governance Publishing

IT Governance Publishing
IT Governance Ltd
66 Silver Street
Ely
Cambs CB7 4JB
United Kingdom

www.itgovernance.co.uk

ISBN 1-905356-11-0

About the author

Alan Calder is the founder director of IT Governance Ltd (www.itgovernance.co.uk), an information, advice and consultancy firm that helps company boards tackle governance, risk management, compliance and information security issues. He has many years of senior management experience in the private and public sectors.

The company distributes a range of books, tools and other publications on governance, risk management, compliance and information security through its website.

Other titles:

IT Governance: a Manager's Guide to Data Security and BS7799/ISO17799. The third edition of this book was published by Kogan Page in June 2005.
A Business Guide to Information Security (Kogan Page and the IOD, October 2005)
IT Governance: Guidelines for Directors (April 2005)
IT Governance Today: a Practitioner's Handbook (May 2005)
Nine Steps to Success: an ISO 27001 Implementation Overview (October 2005)
The NON-Geek Guide™ to Wireless Security (March 2005)
The Internet Highway Code (March 2005)

Other titles are planned for publication during 2006; see the website for details.

Acknowledgement

Some of the material in this book has appeared elsewhere in books and articles by Alan Calder; this is the first time that all the material germane to the Case for ISO27001 has been gathered together in one place, re-purposed and expanded.

CONTENTS

INTRODUCTION

The replacement, in late 2005, of BS 77799-2:2002 by the international Information Security Management System standard ISO/IEC 27001:2005 marks the coming of age of information security management.

In the first eight years that BS7799 existed as a standard against which organizations could gain an external certification, about 1,000 were successful, worldwide. This number doubled in the subsequent twelve months. With the internationalisation of BS 7799, that number will grow geometrically. This books looks at why organizations are increasingly turning to this information security management standard.

By far the most common drivers for organizations that have, historically, been successful in achieving BS 7799, "were commercial: to increase the confidence of customers, or possibly to encourage suppliers, when dealing with the organization."[1] For others, according to the same survey, an information security management standard is "becoming an increasing requirement in tender documents, as well as contracts" and, for a very sizable minority, gaining a competitive advantage over their competitors has been equally important.

Technology – specifically information technology - is transforming the economic and social worlds in which we

---

[1] Information Security BS7799 Survey 2005 – Information Security Ltd

work, play and live. Whether or not this is a good thing is irrelevant. The fact is that, for most people, information was stored, twenty years ago, on pieces of paper. Small numbers of large mainframe computers batch-processed mundane transactions and a credit card application could take several weeks. Corporations wrote their own computer programs and avoiding GIGO (garbage in, garbage out) was the Head of IT's prime objective. Fax machines were transforming a business communication infrastructure that still depended on expensive fixed telephone lines. Information, when it existed, was hard to lay your hands on and even harder to use, manipulate or transform.

Today, 'information overload' is a commonplace complaint. Computers are ubiquitous, communication can be globally instantaneous, and someone else can get a credit card in your name in a matter of minutes.

As we've shifted from a manufacturing to an information economy, the structure of organizational value has changed dramatically. The intangible assets (mostly intellectual capital) of most OECD organizations are now worth substantially more than their tangible assets and this trend is unlikely to reverse.

Information is the life blood of the modern business. All organizations possess and use critical or sensitive information. Roughly nine-tenths of businesses now send e-mail across the Internet, browse the web and have a website; and 87% of them now identify themselves as 'highly dependent' on electronic information and the systems that process it. Information and information systems are at the heart of any organization trying to operate in the high-speed wired world of the 21st Century.

Business rewards come from taking risks; managed, controlled risk-taking, but risk-taking nonetheless. The business environment has always been full of threats, from employees and competitors through criminals and corporate spies to governments and the external environment. The change in the structure of business value has led to a transformation in the business threat environment.

The proliferation of increasingly complex, sophisticated and global threats to this information and its systems, in combination with the compliance requirements of a flood of computer- and privacy-related regulation around the world, is forcing organizations to take a more joined-up view of information security. Hardware-, software- and vendor-driven solutions to individual information security challenges no longer cut the mustard. On their own, in fact, they are dangerously inadequate.

News headlines about hackers, viruses and online fraud are just the public tip of the data insecurity iceberg. Business losses through computer failure, or major interruption to their data and operating systems, or the theft or loss of intellectual property or key business data, are more significant and more expensive.

Organizations face criminal damages, reputation loss and business failure if they omit to adequately secure their information. Directors face loss of personal reputation and jail time if they fail in their duty to protect the information their organizations are holding.

But computer security technology, on its own, simply does not protect information. On its own, it just wastes money, gives a false sense of security and decreases business efficiency. What organizations need is a structured method for identifying the real information risks they face, the financial impact of those threats, and appropriate methods of mitigating those specific, identified risks. Securing information is not rocket science, whatever the technology vendors might say. Information is at risk as much through human behaviour (and inattention) as it is through anything else. Securing information therefore requires an approach that is as much about process and individual behaviour as it is about technological defences.

And no organization has either the time or the resources to try and work out, on its own and from first principles, how to do this effectively. Apart from anything else, the time and error profile is likely to be unattractive.

No organization needs to. ISO27001 already exists. This standard, which contains current information security international best practice that has already been successfully implemented in more than two thousand organizations around the world, gives organizations a reliable and effective framework for deploying an information security management system that will preserve its assets, protect its directors and improve its competitiveness.

This book explains how.

CHAPTER 1: INFORMATION ECONOMY, INTELLECTUAL CAPITAL

Executive summary

In the information economy, businesses depend on information and a substantial proportion of their value is made up of intangible and information assets. The board has a fiduciary duty to protect and preserve these assets.

The information economy

The new information, or knowledge, economy is (as we all know) fundamentally different from the old manufacturing one. Information interchange has speeded up the globalization of markets, products and resourcing. This has lead to increasingly similar shopping streets selling increasingly similar products throughout the developed world. Over 70% of workers in developed economies are now knowledge, rather than manual, workers – including those factory and farm workers whose work depends on understanding and using information technology. Information networking and telecommunications connectivity make this 'global village' possible – and bring a number of specific business threats and challenges at the same time.

The key characteristics of the global information economy, in contrast to those of the older manufacturing one, are:

- Information and knowledge are not depleting resources to be protected; on the contrary, sharing knowledge drives innovation;
- Effects of location and time are diminished – virtual organizations now operate round the clock in virtual marketplaces, and organizations based on East Coast America manufacture in China, handle customer support from India, and sell globally through a single, multi-currency web site;
- Laws and taxes are difficult to apply effectively on a national basis as knowledge quickly shifts to low tax, low regulation environments;
- Knowledge enhanced products command price premiums;
- Captured knowledge has a greater intrinsic value than 'knowledge on the hoof'.

"What's new? Simply this: Because knowledge has become the single most important factor of production, managing intellectual assets has become the single most important task of business."[2]

Intellectual capital

Most people are aware that, for most organizations, the value of their tangible assets – land and buildings, plant and machinery, cash and so on – is different from the value of their intangible assets – the ones not carried on their books. The value of the intangible assets is usually taken, in simple terms, as being equal to the difference between the net book value of the business and its current market capitalization.

---

[2] Intellectual Capital: the New Wealth of Organizations, Thomas A Stewart, 1997

1. Information economy, intellectual capital

In the last fifteen years the apparent value of these intangible assets has grown (in some cases, admittedly, because of the Great Internet Bubble's overvaluation of their shares) and now, in many cases, their value exceeds that of their tangible assets – sometimes considerably. In the information age, an organization's key asset is its intellectual capital: its human resources, retained knowledge and intangible assets. Every organization that has a long term desire to survive and succeed in its chosen market must focus on preserving, protecting, developing, and applying its knowledge assets – its 'intellectual capital' - for the benefit of its shareholders.

Because an organization's intellectual capital is valuable, someone else wants it: you could argue (although most accountants might prefer not to) that the definition of an asset is that it is something valued by more than one person – after all, if no one else wants it, it's not much of an asset. If other people want what you've got, you've got to ensure they don't get it – other than on your terms. You've also got to be sure that assets which you use in your business (even if no-one else knows about or wants them – yet) are protected from destruction or corruption – otherwise your business's operating capability will be hampered.

Managing this risk – preserving and protecting these assets – is a key board responsibility. Intellectual capital and information assets need to be protected so that the organization can continue to exploit them in pursuit of its competitive strategy. Information assets depend, for their productive existence, on information and communication technology. Information security, therefore, is also (but not primarily) about computer security and system security.

ISO 27001

ISO 27001 is the international standard for information security management systems and it provides organizations with best practice guidance for identifying, assessing and controlling information risks in strategic business plans and everyday operational environments. It's *the* essential standard for the information age organization.

CHAPTER 2: INFORMATION, IT AND COMPETITIVENESS

Executive summary

Information security is essential if your organization's productivity and competitive position is to be protected.

Academic research

Academic research[3] largely confirms the view that the growth in western economies since 1995 can largely be linked to the deployment and use of information technology. Studies, and experience, suggest that this growth is sustainable.

Other studies[4], focusing on specific industries (eg finance), concluded that there are circumstances where further IT investment will not provide competitive advantage over other firms in the sector, but that investment is nevertheless essential just to stay in the race.

---

[3] *See (for instance):* 'Information technology and productivity: where are we now and where are we going?' (http://ideas.repec.org/p/fip/fedgfe/2002-29.html), published by the Board of Governors of the Federal Reserve System (US) in 2002

[4] *See (for instance):* 'Examining the contribution of information technology toward productivity and profitability in US retail banking,' (http://fic.wharton.upenn.edu/fic/papers/97/9709.pdf), published by the Financial Institutions Center of Wharton University, 1997

Productivity improvements and competitive edge are the two overwhelming reasons for pursuing IT investment. No board invests in IT because it's fun: the investment has to pay off – even if it only pays off in terms of keeping up with the competition.

It is also clearly the case that there are many new, innovative businesses identifying new ways of deploying information technology, creating new business models that conceivably will destroy many existing businesses. Of course, not all of the new business models will survive but some, like Amazon for instance, force a whole sector to redefine how it does business.

Competitive environment

Survival and success in today's business environment requires inventiveness and adaptation; Bill Gates says: 'Microsoft is never more than two years away from failure.' You've got to innovate, find new markets and products, new ways of adding value. You've also got to execute current strategies flawlessly just to make sure you're still in with a chance at the new ones.

And flawless execution, in the information economy, depends on the productivity and effectiveness of your human capital, your staff. You have to simplify their working environment, remove problems and barriers, and give them the information and information technology tools they need. In the same way that you want any new computer systems to be capable of interacting with the old, so that information doesn't have to be transferred laboriously from one to the other, so you should want new computer systems to work smoothly and efficiently: no data losses, no corruption, no downtime.

And that means that information security ought to be built into your information systems infrastructure from the outset. In order for your people to work productively and effectively with information, they need to be able to get at it, it needs to be there, and it needs to be safe. This means that your default information system security setting ought to be: information availability is preserved (no viruses, no attacker-created system or computer downtime, no data destruction, whether deliberate or accidental), as is its confidentiality (no exposure of information to people who shouldn't see it) and its integrity (no data corruption, whether deliberate or accidental).

Software is imperfect (but industrial machinery also broke down), and it has vulnerabilities that can be exploited or which can cause problems. The speed with which hardware and software evolves means that we are unlikely to stand still long enough for any one hardware and software platform to become completely secure and stable – because, by the time it is, everyone will have moved on to using a more up-to-date (although less secure) alternative.

It simply makes sense, for any competitive business, to take appropriate steps to ensure that its valuable knowledge workers can use its information technology infrastructure without fear or hindrance. Technology should be ubiquitous and safe. ISO 27001 enables you to achieve that.

ISO 27001

In the unsafe information economy, ISO 27001 goes one step further. It tells your potential customers, employees and partners that your information systems are – to a recognizable, externally audited, international standard – safe and secure, that yours is an environment in which they will be able to work productively and efficiently and, because you have proved that you can be trusted with information, that your organization is good to do business with. Information security and reputation go hand in hand.

CHAPTER 3: INFORMATION THREATS

Executive summary

All organizations possess information, or data, that is either critical or sensitive. This information is a substantial component of the organization's intellectual capital. 'Information is widely regarded as the lifeblood of modern business.'[5] 87% of businesses now identify themselves as 'highly dependent' on electronic information and the systems that process it. This information faces a range of threats, some simple, some complex, and all with the potential to significantly damage an organization.

Threats

Threats in the digital world, as in the analogue one, originate with people. These people fall into five groups:

- Criminals (thieves, fraudsters, organized crime);
- Malefactors (hackers, vandals, terrorists, cyber-warriors, some ex-employees and other disgruntled or vengeful individuals);
- Spies (commercial and governmental);
- Undesirables (scam artists, spammers, 'ethical' hackers and nerds); and
- The incompetent, or the simply unaware (staff, contractors, customers and other third parties).

---

[5] Information Security Breaches Survey 2004, from the UK's Department of Trade and Industry

3. Information threats

From an organizational perspective, these people are found both inside and outside the organization (the balance overall is probably 50:50). There are a substantial number of people in each category and, because of the nature of the information economy, they are able to exert an influence out of proportion to their numbers.

The digital threats, and the type of attacks that express them, have the same sort of objectives as they do in the analogue world, but because of the nature of computers, digital data and the Internet, their characteristics are different. These characteristics, as identified by Bruce Schneier[6], are:

- Automation: computers automate mundane tasks; illegal or destructive activity with which someone would struggle to cost-effectively achieve critical mass in the analogue world can be automated. Computers make Denial of Service attacks and large scale junk mail possible, just as they enable 100% surveillance of the Internet communications traffic of any individual or organization.
- Data collection: digital data requires less storage space than the equivalent analogue information and can be more quickly harvested, stored and mined. What can be done will (often) be done and, as a result, massive databases of personal and commercial data now exist all over the world. They make spamming, surveillance and identity theft that much easier.
- Action at a distance: in cyberspace, the bad guys are just a mouse click away; the criminal who is targeting

---

[6] Secrets and Lies: Digital Security in a Networked World – Bruce Schneier, 2004

your network may be based in Chechnya, Moldavia or on a Pacific island. He will be just as effective, quick and silent as a criminal down the road, far harder to trace and arrest than his analogue equivalent, and financially more successful.

- Propagation: the Web enables ideas, skills and digital tools to be shared around the world within hours. It also enables techniques to be widely replicated and a vast array of computers to be linked into any one attack.

Attack categories

The types of attacks that occur in cyberspace are:

- Criminal attacks (fraud, theft and grand larceny, identity theft, hacking, extortion, phishing, IPR and copyright theft, piracy, brand theft, 'spoofing');
- Destructive attacks (cyber-terrorism, hackers, ex-employees, vengeful individuals, cyber war, cyber-vandals, anarchists, viruses);
- Nerd attacks (Denial of Service attacks, publicity hounds, adware); and
- Espionage attacks (data and IPR theft, spyware).

These attacks affect businesses indiscriminately. Well understood software flaws (called 'vulnerabilities', by both the 'ethical' and unethical sides of the hacking industry) are widely distributed through an increasingly always-on Internet of ill-defended computers. Individual businesses are rarely directly or individually targeted in an attack (unless they have very substantial assets are some other significant value to the attacker), but they are nevertheless at risk in an environment where automation, action at a distance and propagation enable an attacker to successfully target a very big number of smaller fish. Why target one computer when you can target them all?

Malefactors know that the majority of smaller businesses have inadequate cyber-protection and they exploit this, for instance commandeering large numbers of unprotected computers in huge zombie networks, to mount large scale attacks on targets, usually for purposes of extortion, and to distribute floods of spam. Defences need to be proportionate.

Large businesses and public sector organizations, who have significant assets to protect or who make attractive, high-profile targets, are directly threatened. Their networks are more extensive and more complex, and the quantity and diversity of people and organizations involved with them so great, that they have to be very systematic in identifying and responding to the more significant threats they face.

ISO 27001

The standard provides guidance on identifying and assessing threats. Not all threats are likely to occur and, for those that are, it is essential to have appropriate defences in place. Appropriate defences can be the difference between success and failure.

CHAPTER 4: INSECURITY IMPACTS

Executive summary

No organization is immune from the complex range of threats to its information assets and technology infrastructure. The financial, reputational, operational and punitive impacts of successful cyber attacks or information security failures are significant.

Types of impact

'Impact' is the consequence of the realisation of a threat. It is usually quantified financially, in terms of the likely loss to the organization. Estimation of likely loss is inexact, but should take into account both direct and indirect costs, including the likely business cost of reputational damage, loss of business, remedial advertising, investigating, closing the stable door, etc.

- Every organization will suffer multiple instances of the abuses and attacks identified in this book.
- Business activity will be disrupted. Downtime in business critical systems (such as ERP systems) can be catastrophic for an organization. However quickly service is restored, there will be an unwanted and unnecessary cost in doing so. At other times, lost data may have to be painstakingly re-constructed and, sometimes, it will be lost forever.
- Privacy will be violated. Organizations have to protect the personal information of employees and customers. If this privacy is violated, there may –

under data protection and privacy legislation - be legal action, penalties and substantial restitutionary costs.

- Organizations will suffer direct financial loss. Protection in particular of commercial information and customers' credit card details is essential. Loss or theft of commercial information, ranging from business plans and customer contracts, to intellectual property, product designs and industrial know-how, can all cause long-term financial damage to the victim organization. Computer fraud, conducted by staff with or without third party involvement, has an immediate and direct financial impact.
- Reputations will be damaged. Organizations that are unable to protect the privacy of information about staff and customers, and which consequently attract penalties and fines, will find their corporate credibility and business relationships severely damaged and their expensively developed brand and brand image dented.
- The reputations of directors will be tarnished and, in extreme cases, board members will face personal fines and imprisonment.

Organisations in a number of important surveys[7] are now significantly more pessimistic about the future outlook for information security breaches, believing that incidents will happen more often in future and be harder to detect.

---

[7] Eg The UK DTI's Information Security Breaches Survey 2004 and the Ernst & Young Global Information Security Survey 2004

4. Insecurity impacts

However,

- One third of large businesses and two thirds of all companies still have no information security policy;
- Processes for keeping anti-virus software up to date are often weak.

As a result, security breaches continue to cost industry worldwide many billions of dollars every year. The fact that the majority of businesses are still spending less than 1 per cent of their IT budget on security – and, consequently, suffering losses significantly in excess of the likely cost of defending against them - reflects severe information security governance inadequacies.

ISO 27001

Deployment of an ISMS developed in line with the international standard of information security best practice is the fundamental step toward effective information security governance, and pays off handsomely in terms of losses averted.

4. Insecurity impacts

CHAPTER 5: 'TRADITIONAL' THREATS

Executive summary

All organizations face a range of threats that have been around – and getting progressively worse – for a number of years. Few organizations have taken adequate steps to deal with them. A conclusion of the CBI Cybercrime Survey 2001 was that 'deployment of technologies such as firewalls may provide false levels of comfort unless organizations have performed a formal risk analysis and configured firewalls and security mechanisms to reflect their overall risk strategy.'

Unless the organization actually has a risk strategy, it's not going to be able to ensure that its cyber defences will meet its requirements.

Viruses and hackers

The magazine *Information Security* carried out an online survey of 2,545 information security practitioners in a broad spectrum of public and private organizations in North America, Europe and the Far East. Although this was carried out in July and August 2001, its findings are still relevant:

- A virus, worm, Trojan or some other form of malware had affected 90 per cent of the organizations – even though 80 per cent of them had antivirus software in place.
- The number of organizations hit by web server attacks doubled in number between 2000 and 2001.

31

5. 'Traditional' threats

Hackers (black hat, white hat, and grey hat), crackers, script kiddies and automated hacking exploits all mean that no computer, no network, and no information asset anywhere in the world is safe. Any computer that connects to the Internet will be 'fingered' by an automated 'sniffer' and 'brute force' or 'dictionary' attacks can, in fifteen minutes, run through every word in the dictionary looking for the password.

There are 120,000 known viruses 'in the wild', with the number increasing daily. Viruses, worms and Trojans propagate globally in minutes and the gap between identification of a software vulnerability and release of the first related exploit has fallen to less than a day – the 'zero day exploit'. Worms and Trojans are ever more virulent; the installation of anti-virus software is not, of itself, an adequate defence. Spyware and adware, the emergent malware issues of 2005/6, are still outside the scope of many anti-virus software packages.

Spam

Spam continues to consume bandwidth and, as spam technology becomes more sophisticated, so spam filtering technology needs to keep pace. With spam reportedly at about 85% of all e-mail, and the fact that one man's spam is another's useful new product information, organizations need an intelligent solution to the 'spam challenge' that protects their resources without disabling their businesses.

Commercial espionage

Every major intelligence organization in the world devotes substantial resources to strategic commercial espionage. The theft of product and marketing information, of contractual and negotiating position intelligence, can dramatically alter the balance in a complex negotiation – and the impact on a smaller company can be even more destructive than on a larger one.

Insider threats

The *Information Security* survey also found that: 'insider security incidents occurred more often than outsider ones, but security professionals were more concerned about securing the external perimeter of the organization than dealing with the internal issues.'

These internal security incidents included installation of unauthorized software at 78 per cent of the participant organizations, use of company computing resources for illegal or illicit communications or activities (such as porn site surfing or e-mail harassment), and the use of company computing resources for personal profit (gambling, unsolicited e-mail or spam, personal e-commerce businesses, etc).

Fraud

Fraud is the most debilitating and destructive of insider security threats and the financial controls that evolved to protect organizations against insider fraud in the pre-digital age are inadequate in the digital one. It is essential that internal control structures evolve rapidly so that disasters of the type that destroyed Enron, Arthur Andersen and Barings can be avoided.

Financial organizations and quoted companies already face significant restrictions on the type (and timing) of information that can be published; modern technology – camera phones, MP3 players, USB sticks, Instant Messaging, peer-to-peer networks, Web chat and Internet blogs – are all capable of outflanking 'traditional' security controls.

5. 'Traditional' threats

Staff

Malicious staff are a key source of information threat. Staff, contractors and sub-contractors who wish to damage an organization can usually do so with impunity, particularly where information security controls are weak and they have adequate access privileges – through, for instance, a system administrator password, a covert channel, or an inadequately partitioned network. Of course, the point of greatest danger is usually after someone has decided to leave, but hasn't yet resigned; the fact that so few organizations have an adequate process for managing information access rights for exiting employees is a root cause of the level of insider destruction to information systems.

Systems failures

Systems failure – whether through incompetence, 'fat fingers' or unpredicted external act – can be enough to severely disrupt or destroy any business. Few organizations have adequate, adequately tested, business continuity or disaster recovery plans. Few organizations, as a result, are able to survive a severe disruption and this simple governance failure can have an incalculable impact on shareholders, employees, customers and suppliers.

ISO 27001

The first stage in the deployment of an ISO 27001 information security management system is the identification and assessment of the threats that might impact the organization, and a prioritization of them based on their likelihood and the potential harm they might cause. Risk assessment ensures that risks are appropriately addressed.

CHAPTER 6: INFORMATION RISK IN LARGE ORGANIZATIONS

Executive summary

The information security risks and regulatory pressures faced by larger organizations are of a different league to those faced by smaller ones. Both the threats and the vulnerabilities are significantly different and, as a result, larger organizations suffer more security incidents than the average: ISBS 2004, for instance, reported that 94% of large companies had experienced an information security breach, compared to an overall rate of 74%.

Threats to larger organizations

The threats, both external and internal, are more significant, and this reflects the perceived depth, quantity and value of the larger organization's information assets, its reputation and profile, and the number of people interested in targeting it. The 2004 ISBS showed that 91% of larger organizations had suffered one or more malicious incidents, compared to an overall figure of 68%. Threats range from hackers through cyber-criminals, organized crime and activists of one sort or another to spies and cyber-terrorists – with the nature of threat being related to the organization's activity.

Each sector has its own niche criminals: phishers target consumer financial services companies; industrial spies target intellectual property companies; activists target those companies they perceive as having an environmental or social impact of which they disapprove; hackers target those companies whose scalp will bring them the most prestige; and cyber-terrorists target those companies through which they think they can inflict the most damage on the West. Fraudsters target any organizations where they can find a way of siphoning off cash, and probably work from inside.

More people are made redundant by, or fall out with, large organizations, and more contractors have their contracts terminated by large organizations – not proportionally, but in absolute terms, and simply because such large numbers of people are employed by any large organization. There are, therefore, likely to be many more people with a grudge against any one larger organization than there against many smaller ones.

Information leaked by a larger company is likely to be more price sensitive than that about a smaller one; details of its strategic plans (including mergers, acquisitions, restructurings, product launches, logistics, procurement, trial results, etc) are likely to have substantially more cash value than similar information from much smaller companies, and large company insiders are therefore more likely to be tempted to try and profit from such privileged information.

And, of course, for regulators and enforcers, targeting one or two non-compliant larger businesses brings a better return on investment than pursuing a number of smaller ones while, for institutional shareholders, the expectation is that larger organizations will be models of transparent, effective corporate governance and compliance.

Vulnerabilities in larger organizations

Paradoxically, larger organizations often have more vulnerabilities than smaller ones.

6. Information risk in large organizations

- Almost all larger organizations have now gone digital: e-mail, employee Internet access and transactional Websites are standard; wireless networking and remote access are being rapidly deployed.
- Larger organizations are more complex: they have multiple divisions and business units (each with its own management and operational ethos, each with sufficient local discretion to take actions that will seriously compromise the parent organization) operating internationally and across multiple jurisdictions, with different products and services and, therefore, different information technology needs.
- Large organizations have often been built through a number of acquisitions, each of which brought a slightly different information technology infrastructure (architecture, hardware, operating systems, applications, bespoke software, working practices, culture, values and philosophy) to the party, not all of which has yet been (or is intended to be) successfully integrated into a single, harmonious whole.
- While every system has its own vulnerabilities, the complexity of the whole creates another series of super-vulnerabilities. Most large organizations also have one or more legacy systems, which individual units or divisions may depend on, and which are no longer capable of integration into the overall architecture and may no longer be supported by their vendors. They work, though, for the moment.

- Their multiple suppliers and volumes of customers all want electronic linkages with the company, and every such linkage is also a point of vulnerability.
- Larger companies are more likely to have outsourced significant parts of their operations; every outsourcing contract is a potential vulnerability.
- There are more people working in larger organizations; this means that there are more opportunities for someone to err, and for that error to have a negative impact on the availability, confidentiality or integrity of the organization's information assets. The 2004 ISBS, for instance, identified the fact that 42% of large organizations had experienced an accidental systems failure and data corruption, compared to an overall rate of just 27%.

Impacts on larger organizations

The impacts on larger businesses are significantly worse than the overall average. According to ISBS 2004, percentages of large organizations, compared to the overall average, for each of the following, was:

- Virus infection and software disruption: 68% against 50%;
- Staff misuse of information systems: 64% against 22%;
- External intrusions into systems: 39% against 17%;
- Computer related theft or fraud: 49% against 11%;
- The total cost of the worst incident, in a larger company, was between £65k and £190k, compared to a range of £7k to £14k overall.

Data protection and privacy regulation in larger organizations

Complex organizations, with diversified or (partially) virtual business models, operating in and across a number of legal jurisdictions, also have more complex regulatory compliance task than smaller ones. While any one regulation (and its related compliance failure) might apply only to a subsidiary national entity, it is the global parent whose reputation is damaged. The more failures, the more damage; in a global marketplace, where information travels at the 'speed of light', such failures can have a dramatically destructive effect. Moreover, it's the larger organizations that are targeted by data thieves and by regulatory 'enforcers' looking for a scalp; smaller ones have less valuable information to steal, and prosecuting them doesn't win headlines or advance a career.

ISO 27001

Clearly, information security and information regulatory compliance is an even more serious undertaking for larger organizations than for smaller ones. ISO 27001 provides a structured framework and best practice guidance that helps any large organization tackle the issues in a structured and comprehensive fashion that will demonstrate, to any court, clear intent to meet regulatory compliance requirements.

CHAPTER 7: ORGANIZED CRIME

Executive summary

Organized crime has taken to the Internet in a big way. Cybercrime forms a significant ongoing risk for all organizations: if it is worth taking action to secure premises, it is even more worthwhile to secure digital business areas.

Impacts of organized crime

A 2001 global study by the UK DTI found that lapses in security policy had cost businesses between 5.7 per cent and 7 per cent of annual revenues in 2000. European businesses alone, it claimed, lost more than £4.3 billion in that year due to Internet-related crime.

PricewaterhouseCoopers's European Economic Crime Survey 2001 questioned 3,400 organizations in both the public and private sectors. 43 per cent of them are reported to have said that cybercrime would be the 'biggest and most dangerous form of criminal activity' in the future. The consultancy firm IDC, on behalf of the global outsourcing business EDS, polled IT directors of 250 companies in the UK, France and Germany and released the results of this survey to the UK press. While half the respondents were 'concerned', 43 per cent said that they had encountered cases of internal information theft.

Europol, the European Police agency, observed in its 2003 report on EU organized crime: 'The establishment of worldwide financial markets, economic globalization, and the creation of the EU common market, have provided good opportunities for organized crime groups.' In section 4.4, the report observes that 'organized crime groups are clearly among the major beneficiaries of technological progress...crucially, the development of cyberspace [has] provided great opportunities and a vast arena in which organized crime groups can operate...High technology crime will continue to represent one of the major areas of crime in the future, paralleling the development of e-commerce and internet banking.'

The US Computer Security Institute (CSI), with the participation of the San Francisco Federal Bureau of Investigation's Computer Intrusion Squad, has now conducted nine annual surveys into information security at the CSI member firms. The results of the most recent survey showed that, in 2004, total financial losses to criminal abuse, across the 269 respondents who participated, was $141 million. While the biggest loss arose from virus attacks ($55 million) and denial of service attack ($26 million), $11 million of these losses was from theft of proprietary information against $8 million for financial fraud and $7 million in laptop thefts. It was clear that nearly half of those who took part in the overall survey were unable (because they had no method of tracking) or unwilling (because of the possible reputational damage) to provide estimates of their financial losses from the successful attacks they had experienced. Equally clear is the fact that incidents of cybercrime originate equally from outside and inside the attacked computer systems.

The conclusions of the Confederation of British Industry's (CBI) 2001 Cybercrime Survey, which polled 154 member firms and found that two-thirds of them had suffered serious computer crime in the previous twelve months, are even more valid today. Nearly 60 per cent predicted that cybercrime would become even more of a problem in the future. The Director-General of the CBI, Sir Digby Jones, was quoted as saying, 'Fears about potential losses and damage to reputation from cybercrime are stalling the growth of e-business, especially for b2b transactions. That growth will only come when all parties are reassured that adequate security is in place to protect them.'

'Over its seven-year lifespan' concluded the CSI, 'the survey has told a compelling story. A sense of the "facts on the ground" has emerged. There is much more illegal and unauthorized activity occurring in cyberspace than corporations admit to their clients, stockholders and business partners or report to law enforcement. Incidents are widespread, costly and commonplace.'

ISO 27001

While deployment of an ISO 27001 ISMS will not stop all criminal activity, it will reduce the instances of criminality inside the organization while increasing the prospects of early identification of crime and a rapid, controlled response that minimises damages and loss.

CHAPTER 8: TERRORISM

Executive summary

Cybercrime is a serious issue. It may be a lesser danger to organizations than the effects of what is called 'cyberwar': cyber war is even less discriminate than criminal activity, but potentially more devastating. Every organization has a role to play in securing cyberspace against terrorist attacks.

Cyber-capabilities

On 12 September, 2001, the US General Accounting Office (GAO) reported that 24 US federal bodies, from the Treasury to the Pentagon, had computer systems 'riddled with weaknesses'. It said that hackers could read or tamper with critical information. On 18 September, the Nimda worm infected and shut down 100,000 computers worldwide within 24 hours. Every significant terrorist or criminal organization is believed to have cyber-capabilities and to have become very sophisticated in its ability to plan and execute attacks using the most recent technology.

Eliza Manningham-Butler, Director General of the UK's Security Service, said this at the 2004 CBI annual conference: 'A narrow definition of corporate security including the threats of crime and fraud should be widened to include terrorism and the threat of electronic attack. In the same way that health and safety and compliance have become part of the business agenda, so should a broad understanding of security, and considering it should be an integral and permanent part of your planning and Statements of Internal Control; do not allow it to be left to specialists. Ask them to report to you what they are doing to identify and protect your key assets, including your people.'

More than 400 million computers are linked to the Internet; many of them are vulnerable to indiscriminate cyber-attack. The critical infrastructure of the First World is subject to the threat of cyber assaults, ranging from defacing websites to undermining critical national computer systems. In February 2003, the White House published the *National Strategy to Secure Cyberspace*, in which the President recognised that securing cyberspace would be an extraordinarily difficult task, requiring the combined and co-ordinated effort of the whole of society and that, without such an effort, an infrastructure that is 'essential to our economy, security and way of life' could be disrupted to the 'extent that society would be debilitated'.

ISO 27001

Every organization has a role to play in society's survival of a terrorist attack, which is to take its own precautions to ensure that it has a reasonable prospect of survival. The standard provides guidelines that, when deployed, reduce the organization's level of exposure to the impacts of terrorist attack while improving its own business continuity arrangements.

CHAPTER 9: EVOLVING THREAT ENVIRONMENT

Executive summary

The current situation is not good, and is unlikely to get better. All boards need to take action to deal with current risks; they also need to ensure that they are able to cope with future ones.

Key trends

A number of significant trends mean that information security will become even more challenging in the years ahead.

- The use of distributed computing is increasing. Computing power has migrated from centralized mainframe computers and data processing centres to a distributed network of desktop, laptop and micro computers, and this makes information security much more difficult.
- There is a strong trend toward mobile computing. The use of laptop computers, Personal Digital Assistants (PDAs), mobile phones, digital cameras, portable projectors and MP3 players has made working from home or on the road relatively straightforward, with the result that network perimeters are becoming increasingly porous. There are many more remote access points to networks, and the fast-growing number of easily accessible endpoint devices increases the opportunities to break into networks and steal or corrupt information.

9. Evolving threat environment

- There has been a dramatic growth in the use of the Internet for business communication, underpinning the development of Instant Messaging, wireless, VoIP, blogging and broadband. The Internet provides an effective, immediate and powerful method for organizations to communicate on all sorts of issues. This exposes all these organizations to the security risks that go with connection to an unregulated environment and deployment, in an enterprise setting, of tools originally designed for consumers – and which have little or no enterprise-strength security capability.
- Better hacker tools are available every day, on hacker websites that, themselves, proliferate. These tools are improved regularly and, increasingly, less and less technologically proficient criminals – and computer literate terrorists - are enabled to cause more and more damage to target networks.
- Increasingly, hackers, virus writers and spam operators are co-operating to find ways of spreading more spam: not just because it's fun, but because direct e-mail marketing of dodgy products is highly lucrative. Phishing and other internet fraud activity will continue evolving and will become an ever bigger problem.
- This will lead, inevitably, to an increase in blended threats that can only be countered with a more effective combination of technologies and processes.
- Increasingly sophisticated technology defences, particularly around user authorization and authentication, will drive an increase in social engineering-derived hacker attacks.

9. Evolving threat environment

ISO 27001

In an increasingly threatening environment, directors need to take appropriate action to deal with the risks to their business from threats to their information and technology assets and infrastructure. They don't have time to re-invent the wheel, to solve the security problems afresh at every organization, nor do they need to. Information insecurity is a common problem and a common, best-practice solution has emerged: ISO 27001 provides a vendor-independent, system-agnostic information security framework that any organization anywhere in the world can apply to help manage its information related risks.

CHAPTER 10: REGULATORY COMPLIANCE

Executive Summary

Today's regulatory environment is increasingly complex, the penalties for failure unattractive and the route to effective compliance not clear. ISO 27001 provides a best-practice solution to a range of regulatory issues faced by directors.

The Regulatory Conundrum

Organizations have traditionally responded to regulatory compliance requirements on a law-by-law, or department-by-department basis. That was, last century, a perfectly adequate response. There were relatively few laws, compliance requirements were generally firmly established and well-understood, and the jurisdictions within which businesses operated were well-defined.

Over the last decade, all that has changed. Rapid globalisation, increasingly pervasive information technology, the evolving business risk and threat environment, and today's governance expectations have, between them, created a fast-growing and complex body of laws and regulations – such as Data Protection and privacy legislation (e HIPAA, GLBA, DPA) and governance requirements (eg SOX and Turnbull) - that all impact the organization's IT systems. While global companies are in the forefront of finding effective compliance solutions, every organization, however small, and in whatever industry, is faced with the same broad range of regulatory requirements.

These regulatory requirements focus on the confidentiality, integrity and availability of electronically-held information, and primarily – but not exclusively – on personal data. Many of the new laws appear to overlap and, not only is there very little established legal guidance as to what constitutes compliance, new laws and regulatory requirements continue to emerge. Increasingly, these laws have a geographic reach that extends to organizations based and operating outside the apparent jurisdiction of the legislative or regulatory body that originated them.

Regulatory requirements in all these areas concentrate on preserving the confidentiality, integrity and availability of electronic data held by organizations operating within the sector. Regulations, which are technology-neutral, describe what must be done, but not how. Organizations are left to establish, for themselves, how to meet these requirements.

In most instances, there is not yet a body of tested case law and proven compliance methodologies to which organizations can turn in order to calibrate their efforts. There are no technology products which, of themselves, can render an organization compliant with any of the data security regulations, because all data security controls consist of a combination of technology, procedure and human behaviour. In other words, installing a firewall will not protect an organization if there are no procedures for correctly configuring and maintaining it, and if users habitually bypass it (through, for instance, Instant Messaging, Internet browsing or the deployment of rogue wireless access points).

In the face of new, blended, complex and evolving threats to their data, organizations have business and regulatory obligations to protect, maintain and make that data available when it is required. They have to do this in an uncertain compliance environment where the rewards for success don't grab headlines, but the penalties for failure do. Fines, reputation and brand damage and, in some circumstances, jail time for directors are outcomes that every business wants to avoid, and wants to avoid as systematically and cost-effectively as possible.

The adoption of an externally-validated, best-practice approach to information security – one that provides a single, coherent framework that enables simultaneous compliance with multiple regulatory requirements - is, therefore, a solution to which organizations are increasingly turning.

ISO 27001

ISO 27001 provides just such a solution. It focuses on the confidentiality, availability and integrity of data and its key precepts and requirements all occur in the regulatory requirements. Implementation of an ISO 27001 framework enables an organization to comply, at one step (and subject to specific documentation and working practices tailored for each individual regulation), with all the core requirements of information-related regulation anywhere in the world.

CHAPTER 11: DATA PROTECTION AND PRIVACY

Executive summary

Privacy and data protection are linked and relatively new business issues that are now a global business imperative. Failure to comply with privacy and data protection regulations can have expensive commercial and punitive consequences.

There are also good business reasons for protecting personal privacy. A successful business in the information economy depends on users having confidence in the confidentiality, availability and integrity of electronic information and communications systems. No trust, no custom.

Data Protection and Privacy

Personal information is increasingly subject to regulation. There is international, foreign and industry specific legislation and regulation. All OECD countries have some form of Data Protection and Privacy legislation and national regulations often overlap, are sometimes contradictory and almost all lack implementation guidance or adequate precision. Nevertheless, customers, staff, and suppliers, tribunals and law courts all expect organizations to be proactive in their efforts to comply.

Originally very specific to the financial services industry, data protection regimes are spreading to all other industries. Technology – for communication, data sharing and data storage – will continue to evolve, creating new compliance challenges.

Privacy and data protection regulations vary from country to country; some are more lax, others stricter. Outsourcing is a potential source of risk, as data protection may be weaker in the outsource jurisdiction. New privacy legislation is proposed or is under way in many countries, including the US. Around the world, companies that want to compete in the global economy will increasingly see privacy compliance as a basic 'cost of entry', rather like corporate governance.

Shareholders don't expect their companies to be in breach of national or international privacy regulations. Customers, staff and regulators are even fiercer. The ChoicePoint[8] and LexisNexis[9] cases should give every CEO sleepless nights: not only does dealing with the aftermath of the attack cost far more than installing appropriate measures in the first place, you still have to install them afterwards.

The consequences of failing to comply fully with data protection and privacy regulations are now so clear that we can't be far off the time when directors find themselves on

---

[8] ChoicePoint, a US data broker registered in Georgia, was attacked by ID thieves who may have accessed 145,000 personal records; it has since then been subject to a US Federal Trade Commission enquiry into its compliance with the law, an SEC investigation into possible insider stock dealing, and lawsuits in relation to both the Fair Credit Act and California state law

[9] LexisNexis is a Reed Elsevier division that provides legal and business information; 310,000 individual subscription records may have been illegally accessed in 59 separate incidents over two years and, under various US laws, all had to receive letters and ongoing support from the company.

the end of law suits for breach of fiduciary duty in respect of data protection and privacy regulation.

OECD Guidelines

The OECD Guidelines on privacy and data protection have become the international legal framework for data protection, both in the OECD (all of whose member states have adopted the guidelines) and in developing and transitional economies.

In 1990, the EU set about creating a framework that would bring the levels of data protection across the EU to a more common level. The EU's 1995 Data Protection Directive established a detailed privacy regulatory structure that EU member states have since then been adopting into national law, having been given three years within which to do so.

EU Regulation

EU Directives have been, and will continue to be, significant drivers of national regulation. The two most important EU instruments are the EU Data Protection Directive of 1995 (note that although the US was declared a 'safe harbour' for the purposes of EU data protection regimes in 2000 only a relatively small number of US companies fall within the 'safe harbour') and the EU Directive on Privacy and Electronic Communications of 2002.

UK Regulation

Each country within the EU has incorporated the EU instruments into its national law. The UK's versions are identified below.

Data Protection Act 1998 (the 'DPA')

This act replaced the UK's 1984 data protection act, which (amongst other defects) had failed to recognize the link between privacy and data protection. DPA requires any organization that processes personal data to comply with eight enforceable principles of what it identifies as good practice.

The DPA (which is also interpreted in the light of the UK's Human Rights Act 2000) is concerned with personal data, and this encompasses facts and opinions about an individual and includes information about the data controller's intentions toward the individual (eg will s/he be employed or not?). Under the terms of the DPA, 'processing' includes storage, and the requirements apply to both electronic data and paper records (if they are contained in a 'relevant filing system'). The precise definitions of what is, and is not, covered have been further complicated by the findings of the 2003 Durant v Financial Services Authority court case and the Information Commissioner's updated guidance (on his website) is relevant.

The DPA covers a number of areas, including CCTV records, web sites and internet activity, recruitment and selection of staff, employment records, staff monitoring (including, for example, checking telephone records or internet use) and information about workers' health.

Failure to comply with the DPA can result in substantial fines for organizations. The DPA creates something known as a section 55 criminal offence for individuals who, in specific circumstances, fail to comply. The DPA only applies if the data controller is established in the UK and/or the processing takes part in the UK; criminals based outside the

EU and operating in breach of the DPA are able to do so with considerable impunity.

US Regulation

The Safe Harbor framework

This allows US companies that are regulated by the FTC and have operations in the EU to receive European personal data. They can comply with the EU Data Protection Directive by adopting the seven Safe Harbor Principles (the compliance standards are certified through the US Department of Commerce and enforced by the US Federal Trade Commission (FTC)) which are set out on the Commerce and FTC Websites and submitting themselves to Commerce department certification.

The Gramm-Leach-Bliley Act ('GLBA')

The 'Financial Information Privacy Protection Act' was passed in 2001. It covers all US-regulated financial services companies, and charges their boards with protecting their customers' personal information against any 'reasonably foreseeable' threats to their security, confidentiality or integrity. GLBA also applies to a wide range of 'non-bank' managers and the Federal Trade Commission (FTC), which is responsible for enforcing the act, requires compliance with both the letter and spirit of the act. GLBA requires directors to develop, draft, approve and implement an appropriate information security program. Each organization is required to determine its own best practice for achieving the objectives of GLBA and what official guidance there is, is inadequate.

The Fair Credit Reporting Act ('FRCA')

The FRCA was passed in 1999. It is designed to 'promote accuracy and ensure the privacy of the information used in credit reports, applies specifically to consumer reporting agencies (such as credit bureaus) and is enforced by the FTC. It is underpinned by a range of state laws.

The Health Insurance Portability and Accountability Act ('HIPAA')

This act was passed in 1996 and took effect in April 2003. It requires healthcare organizations (health plans, doctors, hospitals, health care providers) to protect – and keep up to date – their patients' healthcare records (which includes patient account handling, billing and medical records), in order to streamline health industry inefficiencies, reduce paperwork, make the detection and prosecution of fraud easier, and to enable workers to more easily change jobs, even if they have pre-existing medical conditions. The 'Administrative Simplification (AS) Provisions' state the specific rules that institutions must implement in order to comply with HIPAA; these include rules for EDI, for electronic signatures and for standards of privacy.

The Californian Senate Bill 1386 of 2003

SB 1386 requires any 'state agency or entity' holding personal information about customers living in California to divulge (which means press releases, communications to entire classes of customers, etc) any breaches of security for any databases that hold that personal information (unless the data is encrypted). SB 1386 is being used as the template for similar privacy legislation in other states of the US; the 'unauthorized acquisition of computerized data that compromises the security, confidentiality, or integrity of personal information maintained by the person or business' triggers reputational damage for the data holder.

The California Online Privacy Protection Act of 2004 ('OPPA')

OPPA requires websites serving Californians (irrespective of the website's geographic or jurisdictional location, or that of the organization owning or operating the website) to comply with strict Californian privacy guidelines, including the conspicuous posting of privacy guidelines that themselves must meet strict requirements. This law goes further than the requirements of GLBA and is amongst the first of a rash of similar laws being considered at state level. Penalties and reputational damage follow for organizations that are not compliant and against which a complaint is made, whether officially or by an aggrieved consumer.

APEC regulation

The twenty-one members of the Asia-Pacific Economic Cooperation forum endorsed, in November 2004, a privacy framework that is primarily commercial in outlook. The framework is consistent with the OECD Guidelines and also emphasizes the importance of privacy regimes in a region where many countries have not yet passed privacy protection laws. The framework adopts the EU and OECD definitions of personal information, and emphasizes the benefits of participation in the global information economy; some countries (eg Australia) already have privacy and data protection laws that are more in line with EU requirements than with those of APEC.

ISO 27001

Throughout the OECD, and more recently in the APEC area, in the Americas and in many Developing World countries, organizations are subject to a complex and often contradictory array of legislation and regulations related to information security – mostly related to data protection and individual privacy. ISO 27001 helps organizations comply with these requirements – particularly in jurisdictions where data protection regulation is relatively new and there isn't an established body of case law and local good practice to fall back on. Deployment of the international standard of best practice is always going to stand an organizational board in good stead when faced with a data protection or privacy violation action of any sort.

Similarly, for organizations operating internationally across multiple jurisdictions and facing, therefore, complex compliance requirements, ISO 27001 provides a structured and comprehensive method of minimising exposure to data protection and privacy violation actions in other parts of the world.

CHAPTER 12: ANTI-SPAM LEGISLATION

Executive summary

Unsolicited commercial e-mail is a threat to the availability of networks and information, because of the extent to which it can clog up the arteries of the Internet; it is also the subject of regulation. When it is carrying a payload (virus, spyware, etc) – it can also be a threat to the confidentiality and integrity of that information. Organizations need to take action to defend their organizations against spam and also to ensure that their own electronic marketing is not treated as spam.

Regulation of electronic marketing

One person's spam is another's useful e-mail marketing – and most companies are interested in e-mail marketing, at least at the level of regular newsletters and other updates, all of which could fall within the definition of spam. In the Information Age, as more and more marketing becomes digital (and Instant Messaging, Cellphones and Voice over IP become attractive marketing vectors), so more and more organizations will need to address the issue as part of their overall IT governance approach.

The EU Directive on Privacy and Electronic Communications was passed in July 2002, with a deadline for implementation of October 2003. It set out guidelines for how direct marketing should and should not be done. It placed obligations on the senders of unsolicited commercial e-mail, including the requirement that people be required to opt-in to receive unsolicited messages, that false sender identities and false return addresses should be prohibited, and a genuine opt-out option should be provided. Not all EU countries have yet incorporated this directive into their national legislation and, where they have, it has not always been uniform.

UK Privacy and Electronic Communications Regulations 2003

For example, these UK regulations came into force on 11 December 2003 and superseded the earlier Telecommunications (Data Protection and Privacy) Regulations 1999. The UK's Information Commissioner is also responsible for enforcing these regulations.

The regulations cover use, by telecommunication network and service providers, and individuals, of any publicly available electronic communications network for direct marketing purposes, and any unsolicited direct marketing activity by telephone, fax, electronic mail (which includes text/video/picture messaging, SMS and e-mail) and by automated telephone calling systems. The key right conferred both on individuals and corporate entities is the right to register their objection to receiving unsolicited direct marketing material, and it provides a mechanism for doing this.

The detailed law around data protection and privacy is evolving as cases work their way through the courts.

US CAN-SPAM Act

The US CAN-SPAM Act ('Controlling the Assault of Non-Solicited Pornography and Marketing Act') of 2003 set national standards in the US for the sending of commercial e-mail and requires the Federal Trade Commission (FTC) to enforce its provisions. This act permits e-mail marketers to send unsolicited commercial e-mail as long as it contains: an opt-out mechanism, a functioning return e-mail address, a valid subject line indicating it is an advertisement, and the legitimate physical address of the mailer. The bill includes many other provisions, such as the formation of a national do-not-spam list, and the prohibition of certain email address collection methods. The 'do-not-spam' list idea was not a good one.

Many US states have also enacted anti-spam laws, some of which prohibit sending unsolicited commercial e-mail to state residents unless they have specifically opted-in to receive it.

Enforcement of legislation has been, in most jurisdictions, both weak and inconsistent. This is partly because enforcement is technologically difficult and partly because so much spam originates in jurisdictions beyond the control of any individual state. However, where authorities and affected organizations determine to take action, they do get results, as actions by various ISPs, by Microsoft, the jailing of a number of spammers and the April 2005 bankruptcy of the Internet's third biggest spammer, all demonstrate.

The real anti-spam action, though, is actually being taken by individual organizations. The most effective defences against spam are at the ISP level, the individual organization's Internet gateway, and the individual user's anti-spam filters. These technological defences – which lead to the creation of 'black' and 'white' lists of e-mail marketers – are the key barriers now faced by any organization attempting legitimately to use e-mail marketing as part of its marketing mix. And e-mail marketing works, but it only works for reputable companies if they comply with the law and apply best practice. Target customers have to trust you if they are going to put you on their e-mail marketing 'white list'.

ISO27001

The standard provides guidance for effectively tackling the twin challenges of limiting the impact of incoming spam while ensuring that outgoing e-mail marketing is legal and appropriate.

CHAPTER 13: COMPUTER MISUSE LEGISLATION

Executive summary

Computer misuse legislation is relevant in two ways: authorities and organizations can take action under it against cyber-criminals, and organizations have to ensure they comply with it themselves. Directors can be personally accountable for any compliance failures.

Convention on cybercrime

Computer crime legislation is relatively new. An OECD expert committee recommended, in 1983, that member countries ensure their penal legislation also applied to computer crime. The Council of Europe in 1989 adopted a recommendation from its own expert committee that identified the offences - which should be dealt with in computer-related legislation. Meanwhile, in 1990, the UK passed the Computer Crime Act and, in 2001, the Council of Europe adopted a Convention on Cybercrime that identified and defined internet crimes, jurisdictional rights and criminal liabilities. The Convention, which comes into force in 2005, identifies the following types of crime:

- Offences against the confidentiality, integrity and availability of computer data and systems (illegal access, illegal interception, data interference, system interference, misuse of devices);
- Computer-related offences (computer-related forgery, computer-related fraud);

- Content-related offences (offences related to child pornography);
- Offences related to infringements of copyright and related rights.

All organizations need to be aware of the Convention's provisions in article 12, paragraph 2: *'ensure that a legal person can be held liable where the lack of supervision or control by a natural person...has made possible the commission of a criminal offence established in accordance with this Convention'*. In other words, directors can be responsible for offences committed by their organization simply because they failed to adequately exercise their duty of care. The Organization of American States (OAS) and APEC have both committed themselves to applying the European Convention of Cybercrime. More than seventy countries have enacted, or are in the process of enacting, computer crime laws.

Computer Misuse Act 1990 ('CMA')

The UK's Computer Misuse Act 1990 was designed to set up provisions for securing computer material against unauthorized access or modification. It created three offences: the first is to knowingly use a computer to obtain unauthorized access to any program or data held in the computer; the second is to use this unauthorized access to commit one or more offences; the third is to carry out an unauthorized modification of any computer material. The Act allows for penalties in the form of both fines and imprisonment.

The Act basically outlaws, within the UK, hacking and the introduction of computer viruses. It hasn't been entirely successful in doing so. It initially had a significant impact on the computer policies of universities, often seen as the source of much of this sort of activity. It does have other implications for computer users in the UK. Anyone using someone else's user name without proper authorization is potentially committing an offence. Anyone copying data, and who is not specifically authorized to do so, is potentially committing an offence. It also has relevance for organizations whose employees may be using organizational facilities to hack other sites or otherwise commit offences identified under the Act – not least because the source of any attack could be traced back to an organizational IP address.

The UK's All Party Internet Group (APIG) reviewed this Act in mid-2004, and recognized that it had been ineffective, largely through inadequate enforcement resourcing. It recommended a limited number of changes to CMA and a number of other actions, by other bodies, to improve the legal environment for computer security.

ISO 27001

As computer misuse legislation becomes more powerful, those organizations that have already taken effective action – through deployment of an ISO 27001 information security management system – will be in a position where they are likely to be in line with the requirements of what are likely to be ill-aligned international laws.

CHAPTER 14: HUMAN RIGHTS

Executive summary

Human rights are, in the information economy, an increasingly important issue. They are, of course, important in every other sense as well; however, directors need to ensure that their organizational policies and procedures are compliant.

The UK's Human Rights Act 1998 ('HRA')

The HRA was enacted in October 2000. It incorporated into UK law the principles of the European Convention for the Protection of Human Rights and Fundamental Freedoms (the Convention). Most of the rights within the Convention are qualified, insofar as they are subject to limitations if the employer can show necessity to protect the rights and freedom of others. In particular, an employee could argue in a court or tribunal that the employer monitoring or tapping the employee's work telephone or e-mail or Internet activity was a breach of her/his rights under the Convention.

Regulation of Investigatory Powers Act 2000 ('RIPA')

Section 1 of the RIPA makes it unlawful to intentionally intercept communications over a public or private telecommunications network without lawful authority. Section 3 allows a defence if it can be reasonably believed that both parties consented to the interception. The Telecommunications (Lawful Business Practice) (Interception of Communications) Regulations 2000 (the

Regulations) were issued under the powers of the RIPA and these allow employers to monitor employee communications where the employee has not given express consent, but only under very specific conditions and for specified purposes.

Employers also have to take reasonable steps to inform employees that their communications might be intercepted. This means that employers must introduce Acceptable Use Policies that set out, for the employees, the right to monitor such communications.

Code of Practice

The Information Commissioner published a Code of Practice called 'The Use of Personal Data in Employer/Employee Relationships'. This code is more restrictive than the Regulations issued under the power of the RIPA. There will certainly be a series of court and tribunal cases over the next few years that deal with the conflicts between the HRA, the RIPA, and the Code.

ISO 27001

Deployment of a best practice information security management system is likely to ensure that the organization keeps in line with emerging Human Rights legislation around the world.

CHAPTER 15: RECORD RETENTION AND DESTRUCTION

Executive summary

Legislation, regulation, business contracts and prudence mandate the retention of specific records. These records are largely electronic (including e-mail) and their confidentiality and integrity needs to be protected throughout the period of retention, and they need to be accessible – in spite of intervening technology upgrades and system changes.

Records

An increasingly wide range of organizational and individual records (including e-mail, voice mail and Instant Message communications) must be retained to meet statutory or regulatory requirements, while others may be needed to provide adequate defence against potential civil or criminal action or to prove the (current and historic) financial status of the organization to a range of potential interested parties, including shareholders, tax authorities, auditors and to meet contractual liabilities. Records should be kept in a format that can prove they have not been tampered with, and so that they can be found many years later. This implies that organizations need an effective archive management policy and, inevitably, appropriate technology. Records do not (and should not) be kept for ever – this can make it difficult to find what is required as and when it is required, and the cost of storage is likely to be increasingly expensive.

Therefore, time limits – based, in each instance, on the maximum retention period identified in any of a statute of limitations, relevant legislation (including tax and company legislation) or specific regulatory requirements - should be set for the retention of each individual category of information. Information lifecycle management automates the process of moving information from primary (expensive) to secondary (much less expensive) storage devices. After the defined time period, records should be destroyed – in line with the procedure adopted by the organization to ensure that any confidential information within those records is not inadvertently made public.

Failure to retain, in an accessible format (which might mean retaining versions of all old software and hardware after upgrades, in order to ensure accessibility) key records can have a significant impact on an organization, not just in terms of fines and reputational impact, but also possibly in civil damages.

ISO 27001

Application of appropriate controls, developed in line with the guidelines of the standard, ensures both that data is retained and protected, and that the controls applied to protect retained information are consistent with those deployed for current information.

CHAPTER 16: INFORMATION SECURITY GOVERNANCE

Executive summary

The availability, integrity and confidentiality of its data are fundamental to the long-term survival of any 21st-century organization. Unless the organization takes a top-down, comprehensive and systematic approach to protecting its information, it will be vulnerable to the wide range of threats identified in this book. These threats are a 'clear and present danger' to organizations of all sizes and in all sectors; responsibility for information risk management, for ensuring that the organization appropriately defends its information assets, can no longer be abdicated or palmed off on the Head of IT. The board has to take action. It's a part – and a very key part – of the board's overall governance responsibility. Many (but not all) boards – to date – have shirked, or failed in – this responsibility.

What is 'information security'?

'Information security', according to the internationally recognized code of information security best practice, ISO 17799:2005, is the 'preservation of the confidentiality, integrity and availability of information.'

This book has identified the major information security issues facing boards and management teams and identifies how ISO 27001, the international standard of information security best practice, can give organizations a significant competitive and regulatory edge.

16. Information security governance

Information security is a board responsibility

Information security is a governance issue, not merely an IT department functional responsibility. In an environment where it is not commercially sensible to invest in providing security against every possible risk nor where 100 percent security is affordably achievable, there are five reasons for this:

1. The board has to lay down guidelines as to which of the organization's information assets are to be protected and the level to which this must be done;

2. The board has to prioritize, and lay down guidelines for, investment in information security;

3. Information security is a 'whole business' exercise; effective information security requires a set of controls that integrate technology, procedure and human user behaviour in such a way that the board's security objectives are achieved. Only the board can set out the objectives and requirements for such a cross-organizational management system;

4. The whole organization is at risk in the event of an information security breach (eg LexisNexis); corporate reputation, corporate earnings and corporate survival are the direct responsibility of the board and the board must, therefore, ensure that appropriate arrangements are made to protect the organization from information risk;

5. It is the board's direct responsibility to ensure that the organization complies with the laws of the jurisdictions in which it trades. The growing body of information-related legislation is such that the board now has to be pro-active in mandating the

implementation of a recognised information security management system that will ensure compliance.

Governance and risk management

The board's job is governance and strategy and, therefore, governing strategic and operational risk is a fundamental board responsibility. There are three operational risks (operational risk is 'the risk of direct or indirect loss resulting from inadequate or failed internal processes, people and systems or from external events'[10]) related to information and communications technology that boards need to consider:

1. Loss of proprietary information, with resultant damage to earning power and competitive position;
2. Loss of customer and personal data, with resultant damage to commercial and directors' personal reputations, as well as regulatory action, financial and punitive loss, and possible jail time for directors;
3. Interruptions to business continuity, with resultant damage to commercial reputation and actual trading capability.

Boards have to prioritize the risks that are to be defended against, in the light of the organization's information assets, its business model and its overall business strategy. It has to ensure that appropriate resources are committed to realising and maintaining the risk profile that it has mandated.

---

[10] "Operational Risk", a consultative document from the Basel Committee on Banking Supervision in January 2001

Corporate governance codes

Corporate governance codes throughout the world recognize that the management of operational risk is a core board responsibility.

The UK's Combined Code requires listed companies to annually review '*all material controls, including financial, operational and compliance controls, and risk management systems.*'[11] The Turnbull Guidance explicitly requires boards, on <u>an ongoing basis</u>, to identify, assess and deal with significant risks in all areas, including in *information and communications processes.*[12] Sarbanes Oxley requires US listed companies (and, increasingly, there is a knock-through effect on their major suppliers) to annually assess the effectiveness of their internal controls, and places a number of other significant governance burdens on executive officers, including the section 409 requirement that companies notify the SEC '*on a rapid and current basis such additional information concerning material changes in the financial condition or <u>operations</u> of the issuer.*'

Pillar 1 of the Basel 2 Accord aims to reduce financial institutional '*exposures to the risk of losses caused by failures in systems, processes, or staff or that are caused by external events.*'[13]

Risk assessment has, over the last few years, become a pervasive and invasive concept: a risk assessment must be structured and formal, and nowadays one is expected in almost every context – from a school outing through to a

---

[11] Combined Code on Corporate Governance, Section C.2.1, July 2003

[12] Turnbull Guidance, paragraph 21

[13] BIS Press Release, 26 June 2004

major corporate acquisition. It is certainly a cornerstone of today's corporate governance regimes. In the context of operational risk, a risk assessment is the first step that a board can take to controlling the risk; the most important step is the development of a risk treatment plan (in which risks are accepted, controlled, eliminated or contracted out) that is appropriate in the context of the company's strategic objectives.

Information risk

If no-one else wanted it, it wouldn't be an asset. Information, to be useful to an organization, must be available (to those who need to use it), confidential (so that competitors can't steal a march) and its integrity must be guaranteed (so that it can be relied upon). Information risk arises from the threats – originating both externally and internally – to the availability, confidentiality and integrity of the organization's information assets.

Headline figures dramatically illustrate the cost of security failures: the UK's National High Tech Crime Unit (NHTCU) reported[14] that 89% of firms interviewed had suffered some form of computer crime in the previous 12 months (up from 83% in the previous year), at a cost of at least £2.4bn.

Threats to information security are wide ranging, complex and costly. External threats include casual criminals (virus writers, hackers), organized crime (virus writers, hackers, spammers, fraudsters, espionage, ex-employees) and terrorists (including anarchists). More information security incidents (involving members of staff, contractors and

---

[14] "Hi-Tech Crime: the Impact on UK Business 2005", survey conducted by NOP for the UK's NHTCU

consultants acting either maliciously or carelessly) originate inside the organization than outside it. Baring, Enron, WorldCom and Arthur Andersen were all bought down by insiders. The indirect costs of these incidents usually far exceed their direct ones and the reputational impacts are usually even greater.

The need for determined action to deal with these risks should be self-evident.

Governance failure

The governance failure, though, is evident. An Ernst & Young survey[15] found that only 20 per cent of organizations strongly agreed that information security was a CEO level priority, and that only 24 per cent gave their information security departments the highest rating in meeting the needs of the organization. Ernst & Young summed it up: "ironically, this year's survey seems to echo the sentiments of previous years, as organizations apparently continue to rely on luck rather than proven information security controls. Perhaps the remarkable thing is how little attitudes, practices and actions have changed since 1993 – during a period when threats have increased significantly. Two factors lead us to believe matters have deteriorated. First the threats are more lethal than they were in 1993. What many organizations are slow to recognize is that what they don't know is hurting them and hurting them badly. While scaremongers focus the public's attention upon the external threats with questionable damage guess-estimates, organizations face greater damage from insiders' misconduct, omissions, oversights, or an

---

[15] Ernst & Young's (*www.ey.com/global/content.nsf/International/Home*) 11th annual Information Security Survey, which in 2004 interviewed nearly 1,300 executives across 51 countries.

organizational culture that violates pre-existing policies and procedures.

Second, there is little visible change in how security is practiced by organizations. In 1994, a respondent told us: 'It is apparently going to take a major breach of security before this organization gets its act together.' Some ten years later, that sentiment is still quite evident and typifies organizations' reluctance to do deal with the significant threats and to invoke well-accepted controls."

In today's corporate governance environment, boards simply cannot afford to take their information security governance responsibilities anything less than seriously.

ISO 27001

Implementation of an Information Security Management System that complies with, and is certified to, ISO 27001 is the clearest demonstration that the board can give of its commitment to good information security governance.

CHAPTER 17: BENEFITS OF AN ISO 27001 ISMS

Executive summary

The benefits for an organization in adopting and deploying an ISO 27001 information security management system are three-fold:

1. Cost-effective, fit-for-purpose information security and regulatory compliance;
2. Out-performance vis-à-vis its competitors;
3. Competitive advantage.

Structured Information Security Management System

Information security is a complex issue. Every information asset is subject to multiple threats and the interwoven mesh of related compliance regulation is such that there are no simple solutions. Information security has three key components: technological controls, procedural controls and user behaviour.

The board has to prioritize its approach to information security and commit the investment and resources necessary to achieve its information security goals. It will need to commit certain sums to specific security technologies (anti-virus software, for instance), it will need to mandate the design and implementation of appropriate operational procedures (for updating and auditing anti-virus software deployments, for instance) and it will need to educate and train its staff (so they can tell the difference between a virus hoax and a real one, and know how they are required to respond to each, for instance).

A structured information security management system is based on an ongoing risk assessment process, identifying and classifying risk to organizational assets. It provides best practice guidance on the types of controls (which are procedural, technological and user-related) that might be appropriate for each risk, and provides guidance on implementation. It ensures that inter-relationships between controls and control areas are plotted, so that potential conflicts can be resolved early.

Deploying a structured information security management system ensures that the organization's information security management starting point is a comprehensive and integrated one with complete adaptability.

Benefits of a structured Information Security Management System

"Proving best practice to clients is a contract winner. Many respondents could identify customers and contracts (some worth £millions) that they would not have won without BS7799 registration. BS7799 compliance is now an integral part of many tenders and contracts."[16]

"Companies use registration in their marketing, and many state it gives a competitive advantage."[17]

The benefits of adopting an externally certifiable Information Security Management System are, therefore, clear:

---

[16] Information Security BS7799 Survey 2005 – Information Security Ltd
[17] Ibid

- The directors of the organization will be able to demonstrate that they are complying with the requirements of the Turnbull Guidance, Sarbanes Oxley and/or complying with current international best practice in risk management with regards to information assets and security.
- The organization will be able to demonstrate, in the context of the array of data protection, privacy, computer misuse and anti-spam legislation, that is has taken appropriate action to comply with the laws,
- The organization will be able to systematically protect itself from the dangers and potential costs of cyber attack, computer misuse, cybercrime and the impacts of cyberwar.
- The organization will be able to improve its credibility with staff, customers and partner organizations and this can have direct financial benefits through, for instance, improved sales.
- The organization will be able to make informed, practical decisions about what security technologies and solutions to deploy and thus to increase the value for money it gets from information security, to manage and control the costs of information security and to measure and improve its return on its information security investments.

Boards that fail to tackle information security voluntarily are likely to find themselves forced to it: 'The road to information security goes through corporate governance. America cannot solve its cyber security challenges by delegating them to government officials or CIOs. The best way to strengthen US information security is to treat it as a corporate governance issue that requires the attention of boards and CEOs.'[18]

Benefits of external certification ('registration') to ISO 27001

"The vast majority of organizations had achieved the tangible benefits they were looking for by BS7799 registration. In addition, more than half the participants could identify extra benefits above and beyond those they had set out to gain."[19]

There are a number of direct, practical reasons for implementing an information security policy and information security management system that is capable of being independently certified as compliant with ISO 27001. A certificate tells existing and potential customers that the organization has defined and put in place effective information security processes, thus helping create a trusting relationship.

A certification process also helps the organization focus on continuously improving its information security processes. Of course, above all, certification, and the regular external review on which ongoing certification depends, ensures that the organization keeps its information security system up to scratch and, therefore, that it continues to assure its ability to operate.

Most information systems are not designed from the outset to be secure. Technical security measures are limited in their ability to protect an information system. Management

---

[18] Information Security Governance: a Call to Action – US National Cyber Security Summit Task Force, April 2004

[19] Information Security BS7799 Survey 2005 – Information Security Ltd

systems and procedural controls are essential components of any really secure information system and, to be effective, need careful planning and attention to detail.

ISO 27001 provides the specification for an information security management system and, in the related Code of Practice, ISO 17799, it draws on the knowledge of a group of experienced information security practitioners in a wide range of significant organizations across more than 40 countries to set out best practice in information security. An ISO 27001 compliant system will provide a systematic approach to identifying and combating the entire range of potential risks to the organization's information assets. It will also provide directors of UK and US listed companies, of UK government organizations covered by the government's 'Orange Book' and directors in the supply chains of both public and private sector organizations, with both a systematic way of meeting their responsibilities under the Combined Code, the Turnbull Report and Sarbanes-Oxley, and the wide range of interlocking data protection and privacy legislation to which they are subject, and demonstrable evidence that they have done so to a consistent standard.

It also enables organizations outside the United Kingdom and United States to demonstrate that they are complying with their local corporate governance requirements as well as the data protection and privacy legislation in their local jurisdiction. Equally importantly, an ISO 27001 certificate enables an organization to demonstrate to any of its customers that its systems are secure; this, in the modern, global information economy, is at least as important as demonstrating compliance with local legislation. Possession of a suitably-scoped ISO 27001 certificate enables a supplier to cost-effectively answer the information security and governance questions in request-for-proposal (RFP) and pre-tender questionnaires.

Certification to ISO 27001 of the organization's ISMS is a valuable step. It makes a clear statement to customers, suppliers, partners and authorities that the organization has a secure information management system.

"By far the most common drivers of BS7799 registration were commercial: to increase the confidence of customers, or possibly to encourage suppliers, when dealing with the organization."[20]

---

[20] Information Security BS7799 Survey 2005 – Information Security Ltd

CHAPTER 18: ISO 27001 IN THE PUBLIC SECTOR

Executive summary

Many public sector organizations usually face more significant threat levels than the private sector. All the threats identified earlier in this book apply, but in spades. In addition, many public sector organizations are subject to very specific requirements in terms of information security structures.

UK Public sector organizations

The CSIA (Central Sponsor for Information Assurance) is the UK Government's Cabinet Office unit that is charged with working with the public and private sectors, and its international counterparts, to safeguard the UK's IT and telecommunications services. Specifically, the CSIA role is to provide a central, national focus for information security and its mission includes encouraging the private sector to develop a 'culture of security'.

Its specific aims are to:

'Provide a strategic direction for Information Assurance (IA) across the whole of the UK
Co-ordinate and complement the activities of parties contributing to IA
Sponsor activities that benefit the development of IA

Accredit pan-government systems and in some cases such as the Government Secure Intranet, own the risk to shared information

Identify and address vulnerabilities of national telecommunications systems and progress their resolution through a work programme, in conjunction with government departments or other involved organizations.'[21]

Government departments and other organizations involved in the protection of the UK's critical information infrastructure (finance, telecommunications, utilities and emergency services, etc) include:

National Infrastructure Security Co-ordination Centre (NISCC)
National Hi-Tech Crime Unit (NHTCU)
Home Office
Department of Trade and Industry
Communications-Electronics Security Group (CESG)
The Cabinet Office

All UK central government departments are required to meet internationally recognized information security management standards (e.g. ISO 27001) for their systems. The Cabinet Office's *e-Government Interoperability Framework* (e-GIF) defines the technical policies and specifications governing information flows across government and the public sector. The CSIA has also produced and maintains security framework documents which provide key guidance for both central and local government on providing secure online services, and these are available online from the publications section of the CSIA Website.

---

[21] www.knowledgenetwork.gov.uk/CO/KIMSCSIA.nsf

The CSIA works with other government departments to maintain emergency telecommunications planning and business continuity plans. The CSIA works with business to address the vulnerabilities of public sector and commercial telecommunications systems as well as those of the financial and banking sector.

The public sector collects and holds substantial quantities of data on a daily basis. Some of it is extremely sensitive and personal, and the government is required to protect its confidentiality. Patient health records, social service details, tax returns - all are held on information systems. Private sector organizations also handle personal data and are required to comply with legislation governing the protection of that information.

UK Government departments are also subject to the Data Protection Act, the Human Rights Act and the Freedom of Information Act. This means that government information systems must protect the information they handle and make the correct information available when required, and only for use by those people who are authorized to have access to it. The Department for Constitutional Affairs has published guidance on *Data Sharing in the Public Sector*. (*See* www.dca.gov.uk).

The UK central government has rolled out a secure intranet, the Government Secure Intranet (GSI), for its telecommunications and e-mail services and Internet access. The GSI has been running since 1997. It imposes specific obligations on those organizations that wish to join it. It includes scope for local government and other government agencies to join, with the objective of 'creating a wider-reaching, more secure and joined-up government service'.

The Cabinet Office requires central government departments to appoint a board level Senior Information Risk Owner to be responsible for ensuring that departmental information security procedures are managed appropriately. This means that these procedures need to be based on (but not necessarily the same as – because there are specific central government versions of them) the controls of ISO 27001.

The Office of the Deputy Prime Minister (ODPM) is encouraging local government to meet the same standards. Local authorities were obliged to comply with what is now ISO 27001 by 2005 as part of their *Implementing Electronic Government* (IEG) requirements. There is more information on electronic government on the ODPM Website at www.localegov.gov.uk

Freedom of Information legislation

Nearly sixty countries around the world have passed some form of freedom of information legislation, which curtails government secrecy and requires specific categories of information to be made public in response to specific requests. Another forty countries are reportedly working toward freedom of information legislation. Most countries have an information commissioner who is responsible for monitoring and enforcing the legislation. Usually, only public bodies are covered by such legislation and they can mostly be expected to be compliant with it. Certainly, public sector organizations that defy freedom of information legislation can expect to be publicly pilloried and relentlessly pursued under the terms of the enabling legislation. Private companies, however, should note that one of the clear consequences of this type of legislation (the UK's Freedom of Information Act 2000 is a case in point) is that details of their previously confidential public sector tenders and contracts could now be made public, irrespective of any previous confidentiality clauses.

Board issues in the public sector

A key issue for public sector organizations is to find a balance between the bureaucracy of central government initiative implementation, the likelihood that the organizational board will not have on it any individuals with current or meaningful information security experience, and the fact that central government is an even more enticing target for the world's wrong doers.

CHAPTER 19: IS ISO 27001 FOR YOU?

Executive summary

Unless you're a relatively small organization or, as an organization, you do not use information or information technology, ISO 27001 is an appropriate standard for you to deploy to safeguard your IT infrastructure investments, protect your competitive position and ensure you comply with current and future national and international laws and regulations.

Do you have information that you rely on or which needs to be kept confidential?

If you do, you need to have a structured approach to protecting it against multiple external and internal threats; such an approach requires a mix of technology and procedure, as well as informed and well-trained computer users. The standard contains best practice guidelines on how to achieve this.

Do you collect personal information (eg from customers or employees)?

If you do, you need a structured approach to storing and protecting that information in a way that ensures that your organization is in compliance with a myriad of often conflicting international laws and regulations. The standard contains best practice guidelines on how to achieve this.

Does your business rely on information technology for its daily activities?

If it does, you need a structured approach to ensuring that your systems continue operating without interruption and that your fall-back plans in case of disaster are thoroughly tested and dependable. The standard contains best practice guidelines on how to achieve this.

Do your customers, suppliers or partners need confidence in your information handling and privacy protection measures?

External certification of your information security management system can provide customers, partners and suppliers with the confidence to move forward in dealing with you, knowing that you maintain secure information systems.

Can you afford reputation damage, commercial and punitive losses, business interruption and loss or corruption of confidential information?

Probably not.

If your answers to the first four questions are 'Yes' and to the last is 'No', then you need to deploy a structured information security management system, and as soon as possible. The question that remains is: 'Is ISO 27001 the answer?'

Is ISO 27001 the answer?

The answer depends on the size and complexity of the organization, and the commercial drivers. In practical terms, if you employ fewer than 25 people, ISO 27001 is only likely to be appropriate if you there are specific commercial reasons for pursuing it: you operate in a high risk environment (eg financial services), there is a customer requirement (eg service desk outsourcing services) or some other mandate (eg government or funding requirements). Unless these reasons apply, you will probably be better off pursuing a less complex but relatively practical solution such as the Infosec Basics for Business[22] or even, if you are a very small or home-based business, applying the Internet Highway Code[23].

---

[22] An information security management system for SMEs that is described in *A Business Guide to Information Security* by Alan Calder, published by Kogan Page in association with the IOD in October 2005.
[23] *Internet Highway Code*, by Alan Calder, published by IT Governance Publishing, March 2005.

CHAPTER 20: HOW DO YOU GO ABOUT ISO 27001?

Once the board has recognized the need to deploy a structured information security management system, the steps to implementation are relatively straightforward. There are three preparatory steps that should be taken in every instance.

Preparation

The first is to obtain, and study, copies of both ISO/IEC 27001:2005 and ISO/IEC 17799:2005. It is against these standards specifically that compliance will be measured and they, therefore, have precedence over any other guidance or commentary. Copies of the standards can be obtained from your national standards body or from www.itgovernance.co.uk (IT Governance Ltd is an authorized online BSI international distributor).

The second is to obtain, and study, detailed guidance on how to take the project forward. The only currently available manual that fulfils this function is *IT Governance: a Manager's Guide to Data Security and BS7799/ISO17799*, (the 3rd edition is up to date) which is available from www.itgovernance.co.uk or from most good bookshops.

Thirdly, you need to determine whether or not your ISO 27001 system is to fit in with any other management system (eg ISO 9001) and take appropriate steps to map ISO 27001 components to your existing management system.

Initial planning

The first planning step is a scoping exercise, to determine exactly which parts of the organization should be within the scope of the ISMS, and which not. In larger, more complex organizations, there may be benefits in a staged approach to implementation. Scoping is usually the first part of the initial gap analysis.

Next, you need to carry out an initial Gap Analysis, to identify the gap between your existing information security system and the specification contained in ISO 27001. This initial gap analysis is carried out a high level; its primary objective is to inform your ISO 27001 project plan.

Policy drafting, project planning and securing ongoing board commitment follow; without detailed planning and real board commitment, your project will not deliver the expected benefits and, ultimately, will fail.

Implementation

Once the board is committed, the key project stages are below (and are outlined in substantially more detail in: *Nine Steps to Success: an ISO 27001 Implementation Overview*, available online from IT Governance).

o   A risk analysis and risk assessment, which (if appropriate) is integrated into any existing risk management frameworks or methodologies you may already have. A risk assessment is a systematic consideration of

1. the business harm likely to result to each identified information asset from a range of specific, possible business failures and

2. the realistic likelihood of each such failure occurring

o Identification of the treatment and controls which are appropriate for each of the identified risks (what ISO 27001 calls a Statement of Applicability).

o Generation of the policies, procedures and work instructions that are necessary to document your ISMS, and their integration into any other management system you already have in place. This is the most time-consuming aspect of your ISO 27001 project and you should deploy pre-written policy, procedure and work instruction templates (for instance, the Complete BS7799 Documentation Toolkit – available on download or CD-Rom) to help you cost-effectively accelerate and fast-track this process.

o An operational implementation plan, to bring the infrastructure, processes and competences up to the required standard. This plan may contain a number of individual security improvement programs that tackle specific areas of weakness in greater depth.

o A communication and training plan, to ensure that all users of the IT systems work within the improved information security environment; this should be effectively integrated into your existing HR and training framework and activities. Purchasing and deploying multiple copies of this book can substantially assist in the process of getting organization-wide understanding of the need for an ISMS and the consequent 'buy-in' to the project.

o Internal compliance audit program, to check that each control area has been effectively implemented, to identify and implement possible improvements, and to prepare for certification.

o Selection of external certification organizations and actual certification.

CHAPTER 21: SELECTION OF A CERTIFICATION BODY

Any organization seeking certification will want to be sure that there is a cultural fit between itself and its supplier of certification services, and there will certainly be all the normal issues of ensuring that there is alignment between the desires of the buyer and the offering, including pricing and service, of the vendor. It is completely appropriate to treat the selection of a certification body with the same professionalism as the selection of any other supplier.

There are two key issues that do need to be taken into account when making this selection: the first is relevant to organizations that already have one or more externally certified management systems in place; and the second applies specifically to organizations tackling ISO 27001.

It is essential that your ISMS is fully integrated into your organization; it will not work effectively if is a separate management system and exists outside of and parallel to any other management systems. Logically, this means that the framework, processes and controls of the ISMS must, to the greatest extent possible, be integrated with, for instance, your ISO 9001 quality system; you want one document control system, you want one set of processes for each part of the organization, etc. Clearly, therefore, assessment of your management systems must also be integrated: you only want one audit, that deals with all the aspects of your management system. It is simply too disruptive of the organization, too costly and too destructive of good business practice, to do anything else. You should take this into account when selecting your ISO 27001 certification body, and ensure that whoever you choose can and does offer an integrated assessment service.

The second issue that you should take into account when selecting your supplier of certification services is their approach to certification itself. An ISMS is fundamentally designed to reflect the organization's assessment of risks in and around information security. In other words, each ISMS will be different. It is important, therefore, that each external assessment of an ISMS takes that difference into account so that the client gets an assessment that *adds value* to its business, rather than one that is merely a mechanical comparison of the ISMS against the requirements of ISO 27001

In the UK, the United Kingdom Accreditation Service (UKAS) operates under a Memorandum of Understanding from the Department of Trade and Industry. UKAS accredits the competence of certification bodies – both inside and outside the UK - to perform services in the areas of product and management system approval.

The organization should use only an accredited certification body when seeking ISO 27001 certification. A list or organizations that have achieved BS 7799-2 or ISO 27001 certification, together with the scope of each certificate, can be reviewed at the website of the international user group, on www.xisec.com. A certificate is usually valid for up to three years.

APPENDIX: ISO 27001 – PAST, PRESENT AND FUTURE

ISO 27001 was originally publised at BS 7799, which was the outcome of a joint initiative by the DTI in the UK and leading UK private sector businesses. The working party, which started work in 1992, produced the first version of BS 7799 in February 1995. This was, originally, simply a Code of Practice for IT Security Management. Organizations that developed ISMSs that complied with this Code of Practice were able to have them independently inspected but there was initially no UKAS scheme in place and, therefore, formal certification was not possible. An alternative solution, known as 'c:cure', was adopted to provide a framework for implementation of the standard, and was available from April 1997. The confusion around c:cure and the absence of UKAS accredited certification resulted in uptake of certification to the standard being much slower than anticipated. c:cure was effectively withdrawn as an option late in 2000.

BS 7799 underwent a significant review in 1998. Feedback was collated and, in April 1999, a revised standard was launched. The original Code of Practice was significantly revised and retained as Part 1 of the British standard and a new Part 2 was added. Part 1 was re-titled 'Code of Practice for Information Security Management' and provided guidance on best practice in information security management. Part 2, titled 'Specification for Information Security Management Systems', formed the standard against which an organization's security management system was to be assessed and certified.

BS 7799-2 underwent a further review during 2002 and a number of significant changes were made. BS7799-2 'forms the basis for an assessment of the Information Security Management System (ISMS) of the whole, or part, of an organization. It may be used as the basis for a formal certification scheme'. It is, in other words, the specific document against which an ISMS will be assessed. The 2005 revision of ISO/IEC 17799 (*see below*) led to a change in the controls which was reflected in the new international version of the standard, ISO 27001.

As a Code of Practice, BS 7799-1 took the form of guidance and recommendations. Its foreword clearly stated that it was not to be treated as a specification. It became internationalized as ISO/IEC 17799 in December 2000. BS 7799-2, on the other hand was internationalised as ISO/IEC 27001:2005.

ISO/IEC 17799

In 1998, when the original BS 7799 was revised for the first time, prior to becoming BS 7799-1, references to UK legislation were removed and the text was made more general. It was also made consistent with OECD guidelines on privacy, information security and cryptography. Its best practice controls were made capable of implementation in a variety of legal and cultural environments.

In 2000, BS 7799–1:1999 was, as indicated above, submitted as the proposed text of an international standard and was re-issued with minor changes as BS ISO/IEC 17799:2000. In the UK, it also has the dual number BS 7799–1:2000. It was issued as a single-part standard, titled

'Information Technology – Code of Practice for Information Security Management' and replaced BS 7799–1:1999, which was then withdrawn. BS 7799–2:1999 was then replaced by the 2002 version and this, with the revised Annex A, is the standard against which an ISMS has been certified for the last three years.

The reason for developing an international standard on information security management was described by BSI, on their website, as follows: 'many organizations have expressed the need to have a common standard on best practice for information security management. They would like to be able to implement information security controls to meet their own business requirements as well as a set of controls for their business relationships with other organizations. These organizations see the need to share the benefits of common best practice at a true international level to ensure that they can protect their business processes and activities to satisfy these business needs.'

In other words, the ISO 17799:2005 Code of Practice is intended to provide a framework for international best practice in Information Security Management and systems interoperability. It also provides guidance, to which an external auditor will look, on how to implement a certifiable ISMS. It does NOT, as the standard is currently written, provide the basis for an international certification scheme.

Links to other standards and regulatory frameworks

ISO 27001 was designed to harmonise with ISO9001:2000 and ISO14001:1996 so that management systems can be effectively integrated. It implements the Plan-Do-Check-Act (PDCA) model and reflects the principles of the 2002 OECD guidance on the security of information systems and networks.

ISO 27001 implicitly recognises that information security and any Information Management Security System (ISMS) should form an integrated part of any internal control system created as part of Corporate Governance procedures and that the standard fits in with the approach adopted by the Turnbull Committee.

2005 versions of the standards

ISO/IEC 17799:2000 was significantly revised and published in June 2005 as ISO/IEC 17799:2005. It will in due course, probably 2007, be re-numbered as ISO 27002, to demonstrate that it is in the same family as ISO 27001.

END PAPERS

Useful websites

IT Governance Ltd (the company)
www.itgovernance.co.uk

Blogspot
http://alancalder.blogspot.com

ISO 27001 certification organizations

United Kingdom Accreditation Service
www.ukas.com

BSI
www.bsi-global.com

Bureau Veritas Quality International (BVQI)
www.bvqi.com

DNV Certification Ltd
www.dnv.com

Lloyd's Register Quality Assurance Ltd (LRQA)
www.lrqa.com

National Quality Assurance Ltd (NQA)
www.nqa.com

SGS Yarsley
www.sgs.com

Governance

(US) Corporate Governance
www.corpgov.net

(UK) Department of Trade and Industry
www.dti.gov.uk

European Corporate Governance Institute
www.ecgi.org/index.htm

Internet Watch Foundation
www.iwf.org.uk

National Association of Corporate Directors
www.nacdonline.org

(UK) Office of Government Commerce
www.ogc.gov.uk

Project Management Institute
www.pmi.org

Information security

(UK) Alliance against Counterfeiting and Piracy
www.aacp.org.uk

Anti-phishing Working Group
www.antiphishing.org

(UK) Communications – Electronics Security Group
www.cesg.gov

Carnegie Mellon Software Engineering Institute Computer Emergency Response Team (CERT) Coordination Centre
www.cert.org

Computer Security Institute
www.gocsi.com

Useful websites

Computer Security Resource Clearinghouse (US National Institute of Standards and Technology)
http://csrc.nist.gov

(US) Federal Computer Incident Response Centre
www.fedcirc.gov

(UK) Federation Against Software Theft
www.fast.org.uk

Forum of Incident Response and Security Teams
www.first.org

GCHQ, Cheltenham
www.gchq.gov.uk

(US) General Accounting Office
www.gao.gov

Information Commissioner
www.informationcommissioner.gov.uk

ISMS International User Group
www.xisec.co.uk/xisec/index.html

Information Systems Audit and Control Association
www.isaca.org

Information Systems Security Association
www.issa.org

Institute for Internal Auditors
www.theiia.org

Internet Security Alliance
www.isalliance.org

(UK) National Infrastructure Security Co-ordination Centre
www.nisc.gov.uk

(US) National Infrastructure Protection Centre
www.nipc.gov

Useful websites

The SANS Institute
www.sans.org

(UK) Patent Office
www.patent.gov.uk

Printed in the United Kingdom
by Lightning Source UK Ltd.
116874UKS00001B/292-315